SURVIVAL!

SURVIVAL!

A BOOK OF EVERYDAY VERSE

V Jean Tyler

First published in 2008 by:
Heronslake Hertz

ISBN: 978-0-9543822-4-7

Printed and bound in Great Britain by:
Limited Editions, Remus House, Coltsfoot Drive, Woodston,
Peterborough PE2 9JX

DEDICATION

To a caring and supportive family

ACKNOWLEDGEMENT

To Proprint for their help and advice

To First Thursday Writers' group
For encouragement and criticism

BY THE SAME AUTHOR

'Flashback'	December 2002
'Grains of Sand'	January 2004
'Release'	March 2005
'Going It Alone'	March 2008

Crutchetting on

INTRODUCTION

Independence Day, July the fourth of 2007 found me being admitted to Lundy Ward, North Devon District Hospital for my second hip replacement. The limited mobility before and after the operation precluded my usual physical activities, and gave the time to think and scribble.

I wrote up holiday diaries of my first seven annual 'fix-it' January adventures for publication. A few faraway places poems floated out of this exercise and then the rhyming habit took over the surgical interruption of my life!

I have included the 'first round' poems, published in 'Flashback' in 2002 and then added the recent 'repeat performance' experience. The collection also includes some old favourites (of mine and other people's!) and a wide selection of new poems.

CONTENTS

First Time Round

Repeat Performance

Action Stations

Recovery

Animal Comforts

Family Affairs

Anno Domini

Dreaming And Supposing

Bits Of Heaven

FIRST TIME ROUND

ADMISSION

They put me in a side ward
With a red brick wall to view
And a window from the office
Not quite curtained through

So the light shone in my eyes
When the ward was dark and dorm
I pulled up well the counterpane
And then got far too warm

Sister came and plumped my pillows
I'd been on the brink of sleep
Counting weeping willows
And Devon Longwool sheep

A girl groaned long, nurse called
The orthopaedic team
But later on I sunk into
A deep contented dream

And then, would you believe?
A sleeping pill prescribed
Was noisily presented
I woke and nearly cried!

They are all so attentive
I've not argued or denied it
But for what I'm looking for
I guess you must go private!

DANGEROUS PACKAGE

'Prempak C, now what is that?
Green Senior Houseman queried
'HRT,' I said again
In monotone and wearied

(This was the third time I'd explained
To doctors of all strata
Of orthopaedic speciality -
Who was their alma mater?)

'Hormones to replace those
The menopause can lack'
'Hormones,' he said wide-eyed
'Let me see the pack'

I fumbled in my handbag
Produced the foil-wrapped gems
He scrutinised it well and said
'These can create problems'

He held them by the corner
With deep and furrowed frown
He flared and twitched his nostrils
Then really went to town

'You should have stopped six weeks ago
The surgeons all say thus
You'll get thrombosis, clots you know
And die of embolus!'

Oh how ignorant they are
These men, they think like clones
Do they never read the journals? -
Except the ones on bones.

The Consultant had been different
He had seemed to know
At least the fact that HRT
Restores the status quo

But the Houseman was quite adamant
He took away the pills
And liaised with his superior
My Surgeon, Mr Mills

Who said of course to stop
Would be an outright folly
So Prempak came round daily
On the squeaky medicine trolley

I hesitate to call the youth
A blinkered stubborn berk-
(or could it be he realised?!
HRT might shrink his work?)

A dearth of osteoporosis
In the years ahead
Might so limit his lists
His career could be as read

(This encompasses opinion
In nineteen ninety one
But sixteen years later
Time and knowledge have moved on!)

HERE AND NOW

This morning I know fear
I've got the hippy shake
My pulse is inter-city
My ache's become a quake

I've never been anaesthetised
No, not in my whole life!
Nor has any surgeon
Ever cut me with a knife

Suppose it all goes wrong
And I lose my hippy leg
(I bet that's happened once)
And I end up with a peg

Perhaps I'm hypersensitive
To that epidural
So I'll never walk again
Or roam the world in plural

I've waited for this treatment
Through many a painful bout
But now I look for reasons
To leave and chicken out

The very worst to happen
Would be I'd wake up dead
The list is running late
Great, here comes my pre-med!

NIRVANA

Pills and pillows
Restless billows
Wills and will-o'-the wisp
Strips and stains
Drips and drains
Whiteness done to a crisp

Cleanliness
Light-headedness
Copious analgesia
Distant pain
Felt again
After anaesthesia

Life in limbo
Arms akimbo
Limp dependant tubes
Artificial
Sacrificial
Unsupported boobs

I must wait
In this state
Entering the world
Trust my carers
Health repairers
Till my brain's unfurled.

DAWN CHORUS

'Wakey, wakey, half past six
Drink a cup of tea
I am going off duty now'
Nurse says cheerily

'Wash your top half dear'
(Another nurse has brought her
Trolley with a bowl
Of simply boiling water)

A flannel slop around
A towel pad and dab
Puff the magic talcum
Spray the Cologne fab

Now I am prepared
To face the thin brown toast
With some sticky marmalade
And the morning post

Morning rush-hour follows
Staff skitter fore and back
Rose collects the tray
Maude the refuse sack

A buxom blonde in blue
Plumps in with the hoover
Bangs around the beds
Not a dainty mover

Another comes in mauve
Asthma and lordosis
(HRT when younger
Stays osteoporosis)

She's very gruff in countenance -
And voice too - says she'll spend
All her money on her smokes
With none to leave or lend

I favour the auxiliaries
In their coffee check
Cheery, charming, clearing up
The ward's clinical deck

The routine chores are theirs
They get on and whistle through
All areas in their care
Know what they have to do

The nurses in their role
Have skilled jobs, to dress
The wounds, do drips and drains
Less time to talk I guess.

HIPPY HINTS

Make sure your nightie's not too fine
Remember you'll be taken
With halting steps right up the ward
Your muscles to awaken

A faltering gait in later years
In full glare of the light
Showing body line through muslin
Is not a pretty sight

Make sure your nightie's not too long
There danger lies in store
You need only to crutch once wrong
To sprawl across the floor

Wear a gown with pockets
To walk recovery stage
To carry sweets, pens, dockets
Hands otherwise engaged

By all means look attractive
But it would be a pity
To forego practicalities
In order to look pretty

EUPHORIA

They've done my hip replacement
And I'm still alive
That pain has gone already
I've walked up to Ward V!

GASTRIC RUMBLES

Curry and rice today
But the rice looks more like maggots
And the small bundles of meat
Resemble ties of faggots
However I am hungry
And the flavouring's quite good
Presentation not so vital here
As Floyd on 4 on food!

MOVE!

The physio's here, get ready
Get up, get out of bed
Be bold, be brave, adventurous
And swing that leg of Pb

She's short, in white, she's agile
Her hair is cropped and chaste
Her hands are firm, supporting shoes
Black, sensible and laced

Stand up straight, keep breathing
Place the crutches first
Bad leg, good leg, crutches
Try a second burst

Proceed around the bed
Crutches, bad leg forward
That's good, good leg again
Then halfway down the ward

Grim, but grin and bear it
Turning can be tricky
Circle slow with little steps
Low bowling, wicket sticky

Now for the homeward straight
The best bed is in sight
Exertion so exhausting
Gives dead sleep for the night

PATIENT POSTURE

Arthritic pain has gone
But a dull confounded ache
Spreads down my leg and round my back
Hardly a piece of cake

I wriggle this way and then that
To try and get some ease
Then sister spots my posture
'Uncross your legs now please!'

I uncross them right away
I've been told of this before
It's an automatic comfort
I've indulged for evermore

I turn to lessen pressure
Use my good leg as a guide
And find blessed relief
Hear 'Don't turn on your side!'

I try another pillow
Rotate to fix its place
'You must not turn about like that'
I nod with humble grace

The physio said to move my toes
My ankles, knees and hips
She intended muscle tightening
Not full turnover flips

So it seems I must lay straight
And stay upon my back
Possess my soul in patience
Something I know I lack

They say it soon improves
With each long day that goes
I must attest now I can rest
And take a painless doze

The dark drear nights are longest
The early tea sublime
One was longer than the rest
For British Summer time!

HOME AGAIN, HOME AGAIN, CRUTCHETY CRUTCH

I've made it, I'm at home
My crutching's quite a feat
My hip is settling down
Like the top-up toilet seat!

At first the leg seemed long
(The one with the new hip)
Nurse said 'That's illusion
You've had a pelvic tip.'

Not a pleasant phrase
An unfortunate connotation
It worried me for days
But now the slant sensation
Has completely disappeared
So full marks to the nurse
Two legs of matching length
Are easier to reverse

I've conquered all the stairs
Going down and up
My crutches come in useful
For controlling Tacker pup
Who has a taste for rubber
Bites wellies, chases tyres
And even rubber soles
Of trainers he admires

Yet the crutches' rubber feet
Discourage his attention
A chance for his life training
Of true rubber abstention.

CANINE CONFUSION

Dear Tacker, I still love you
I haven't really changed
Become a doggy hater
Or totally deranged

I've had a hip replacement
A brand new ball and socket
So I have to carry crutches
And the world inside my pocket

When you are your most charming
And expose your ticklish tum
I cannot bend so please don't send
Your shriek to split my drum

Just be patient and bear with me
Another month or two
I'll tickle you and scratch your ear
And make it up to you.

CRUCIAL

Stick insects ont l'habitude
Of thin uncovered limbs
They move with slow stability
And sip their summer Pimms

Their bodies are in simple form
A set of jointed sticks
Straight bits deftly angled
A co-ordinated fix

I love to watch their swinging gait
A slender pleasing pattern
I guess the insect musical
Could use one as a baton

But my sticks are acquired
Just temporarily, I trust
Extensions aluminium of
My upper limbs, non-rust

They are absolutely crucial
Give strong support, but light
For my hourly constitutional
Throughout the day and night

I've learned to swing along
I keep my balance steady
Not as gainly as the insect
But success has made me heady.

REPEAT PERFORMANCE
                              THE WAITING GAME

IN LIMBO

The longer I've waited
 The more time's been dragging
I need op 'updated'
 I have done some nagging
Months are a lifetime
Last weeks even longer
To keep on the move needs
A will even stronger
But now it's to happen
My admission day
The 4th of July,
What else can I say?
Suggests independence
Back in my own home
Optimistic a date then
For coping alone!

BEARING THE WEIGHT

I was just about coping - well really
I could do what I ought to, - well nearly
Like washing myself, the dishes, the clothes
Getting a meal, you know how it goes
But I was all the time, unhappy and sad
The pain was increasing and got really bad

Kind friends called to say 'hello'
But I had to get to the door somehow
Which took me for ever, I'd got so slow
They'd bring me fruit and bunches of flowers
When they'd gone, it took me for ever in hours
To arrange them in a vase or bowl
Minimal movement being the goal
It's tricky with crutches, you have no free hands
To carry a thing so I've stitched two strong strands
To a flexible bag to hang round my neck
(Came free on a cruise when I used it on deck)

Another three weeks before operation
Hope I'm called early to surgical station
If someone falls ill, drops out, drops down dead
So that I can be offered an earlier bed

I do wonder about marching round on two limbs
Like good Christian soldiers in all the old hymns
Darwin's much-followed theory of evolution
Presented the route to the upright solution
But - blasphemous thought - did the Almighty make
To give us a view, a postured mistake?
There's little arthritis in breeds that have paws
I think humans should still walk around on all fours.

THE SPECIAL SEASON

This is June for goodness sake
What's happened to the sun?
Have we had the longest day?
Oh yes, it's been and gone

Each day is rain and greyness
Not even a suggestion
Of that seasonal 'flaming'
What's happened? - that's the question

Some talk of global warming
Which it's said will bring more rain
But wait, the sun's come out
There's summer hope again

But it doesn't last
It's very temporary
Oh of course, rain is essential
This week is Glastonbury!

A NEW OUTLOOK

This is a new experience
Suddenly I can't cope
Each day is getting worse
I've now run out of hope
I cannot work, I cannot walk
This sad hip rules my life
With disablement which pains
And cuts through like a knife

It takes a full ten minutes
To make tea in a cup
To move enough to get the milk
The sugar, I give up
But I'm thirsty, I need something
Oh what state I'm in
-Of course! - it's so much quicker
To pour a glass of gin!

AWAY FROM HOME

I'm staying with my younger son until my operation
It's good to have his family for life and conversation
Their home is new extended, has pleasant country views
While I have left my house, for others to peruse

My neighbours are a great bunch available when needed
Pleasant, sociable, good friends, all in their way succeeded
In their separate lives

Now I'm temporarily disabled, I look to them for help
Of neighbourly support, there's always been a wealth
Especially from the wives

Ex-butcher/farmer David now has a broken leg
Slid down a slippery slope, then by mobile had to beg
For family assistance

(He was videoing some badgers in nearby Peagham Barton
Heavy rain had made thick mud, but he had set his heart on
Filming their existence)

His wife Ann walked her dog each day through my drive
Now has a swollen knee, so it's hard to contrive
How to exercise

She feeds my noisy guinea fowl when I am away
And waters greenhouse plants in the summer every day
With none to supervise

So here's one local family who have problems of their own
And I'm inflicting more stress while I'm away from home

Another neighbour Michael with electric expertise
Did a sponsored walk, a trial for his knees
Which quite gave him the hump

He's still limping and hobbling, can't indulge in bee-pop
Wearing a pirate's eye patch, just below the knee cap
But he'll watch my water pump

(His wife also hurt her knee but she made little fuss
After all, she is a woman, uncomplaining, one of us!)

John who lives right opposite, seemed well and in good nick
But things aren't what they seem, his neck has got a crick
E'en so he has promised to watch my place for harm
And listen conscientiously for that burglar alarm

And as for all my sheep, special Devon Longwool strain
My professional neighbour shepherd has offered once again
To keep a wary eye

Richard will watch and water them, give them ewe nut feed
Take them back to Moortown should there be the need
As the time goes by

How fortunate I am to have these girls and men
I promise when I'm better, I'll do the same for them.

LES JEUNES FILLES

I know two girls, they're sisters
One's Gina, one is Izzy
They have a lovely life
And enjoy being so busy
There's Brownies and there's keyboard
Ballet, jazz and tap
All at different places -
You need a local map
To find the way to classes
Along the country lanes
Not been so well explored
Since invaded by the Danes!

The keyboard is exciting
Not only to play tunes
But to add such a variety
Of rhythmic timing booms
So that for 'coming round the mountain'
She can march or waltz or run
Depending on which time stop
The player switches on

And rhythm is the thing
Look at the way they dance
Floating movement for the ballet
Whenever there's a chance
To practice in the kitchen
In the lounge or hallway
With a sensitivity
Akin to that of Galway

The jazz can be quite startling
The movements strong and sharp
With rapid body twists
Like a fleeting carp

The Brownie Pack is more sedate
With points for really knowing
The motto, law and promises
And mastering some sewing

All these pursuits are wonderful
And keep them very fit
Thank goodness for their mother
(And Dad who does his bit)
For chauffeuring them somewhere
Nearly every day
And collecting others
Positioned on the way

So - hail after school activities
Lucky kids no doubt
I hope I live long enough
To see how they turn out!

HAITUS

There's no one about just now
I'm here on my own
There's comfort and it's lovely
But nowhere's quite like home

The garden's full of colour
Roses of all hues
Crimson, red and yellow
Impossible to choose

Foxgloves show their height
By Buddleia still in bud
A Fuchsia hangs its blossoms
Near a Prunus hood

The inside's very welcoming
A carpet of warm red
Continued up the stairs
Inviting me to bed

Sleep is a great escape
Diminishes the waiting
For the orthopaedic bed
In two weeks' time by dating

Fuchsia Blossoms

THE LEARNING CURVE

I've been hearing Freddie
With his work at home
Homework as they call it
Fred gets quite a tome

He chose his 'family'
To write about in French
And relayed it orally
By the front hall bench

He moved on to Geography
With a different slant
Climate zones in France
Then Global Warming rant

Next Sciences which embraced
Elements and mixtures
And compounds whose components
Are everlasting fixtures

The Maths seems pretty difficult
For me, the old grandmater
But these days they have aids
Such as the calculator

The History was colourful
I love the Civil War
The last battle in Torrington
Knocking at my door

The King and Oliver Cromwell
Fought continuing cycles
Killing many on each side
And blowing up St Michael's

My favourite, his English
A professional review
Of a brilliant film
U must C Ice Age 2

He named the wondrous animals
Symbolic parts they played
Spoke of the camaraderie
When they were sore afraid

To parents he said 'Take your kids
So that their minds will range
To understand and try to stop
Disastrous climate change'

Today exams will finish
How happy he will be
Results at end of term
Time will tell, we wait
And see!

A NOTE IN TIME

Fred's Grade 3 clarinet is scheduled for next week
Pieces, scales, arpeggios, the whole lot so to speak
It seems this vital fact from his mother's been concealed
He declares he told her but she doesn't yield
Now there are just four days to make it for this grade
And practice has been minimal, absent, long-delayed

He collects the instrument from his upstairs room
And starts with minor scales, plays B flat a mite too soon
Up D minor's second octave before he's played the A
But five minutes' application and he's up and away

Arpeggios come next, they're correct if rather slow
But he's concentrating seriously and he knows that I know
If he tries to skip one and slide on to another . . .!
This is my Granny role but I feel more like Big Brother

Then there are the pieces, one with a pleasant cheery beat
Another called 'Lament' slow dreary sad retreat
The third I've yet to hear, last night he had to do
Something more important at a boys' own rendezvous!

SIDE BY SIDE

Upright Yellow Loosestrife
Pinks of Persicaria
Opportunist Pennywort
All in a small walled area

Red Campion creeps between
Inviting opened flowers
Of white Canterbury Bells
In front of Bracken towers

Gentle Alchemilla
Sparkling after rain
Shaken by the breezes
But the diamonds remain.

PRESENTS IN THE AFTERNOON

It's peaceful here this morning
The family's gone to school
Their Mum's at her aerobics
Her Wednesday morning rule
I've written letters and some cards
And done a bit of sewing
Repairing children's clothes
Then I intended going
To the sitting room
For the news on Radio 4
At crutchetting slow pace

But now the postman's at the door
So I travel that direction
- Is there something to pay?-
No it's parcels for young Izzy
Who is six today!

(It has been decided
Her birthday's *after* tea
With leisure time to open gifts
With all the family)

WOLFIE WINS

Freddie's friend is Wolfie
Who lives just down the lane
He came to use the internet
And then came back again

He's something of a specialist
In high class cycle gear
Desperate to update his bike
To use and race this year

The stuff was quite expensive
But this, the cheapest route to get it
He asked for Freddie's mother's card!
. . . I'd have said 'forget it'!!

But she's tolerant and kind
And trusting - and believing
That all will be refunded
The cash she'll be receiving

Next evening Wolfie came
Smiling happy creases
He had the parts and carried
A bag of £1 pieces!

ON HOLD

I'm waiting here till next week
In fact a week today
I should be in the theatre
While surgeons bang away
In ridding me of Right hip one
To give me Right hip two
Now such an encumbrance
There's little I can do

He does four in a day I think
I wonder where I'll come
Anywhere will be good news
- But I fancy number one!
My Left one is quite wonderful
Done sixteen years ago
I hope for a repeat
Of the same get up and go

Last time I well remember
Coming round was bliss
That pain had travelled off
Something I didn't miss
Thank God for anaesthetics
To make me unaware
Of engineering clatter
Pain and small talk which could scare

I'm so glad I was born
In nineteen thirty two
Two generations earlier
Surgeons didn't do . . . . .

                    this operation.

A DIFFERENT VIEW

I sit in a bay window with a valley view of green
Fresh in summer rain, idyllic country scene
Brave young swallows leave their nests after they've been fed
Cheep in the wide world, then when it's time for bed
Respond to parents' summons at dusk to take their rest
Return to snuggle down in the family nest

Mature swaying trees, full-leaved but clearly showing
The very first 'June drop' on the wet grass, overflowing
With carpets of wild flowers, Silverweed and golden glowing
Buttercups and Dandelions

A naked telegraph pole protrudes like a sore thumb
Provides perch for the Woodpecker, a male Red-spotted one
Which clings with powerful feet, its head leaning well back
And takes repeated trips, a long circuitous track
With halts for powerful pecking

A lithe long-legged hare, seen often here of late
Turns its head, twitches its nose and Springbocks through the
gate
How I envy its agility to race across the ground
Stop, listen, then take off again with the speed of sound

To have the time to sit about quietly and stare
Is something I've neglected: solitude is rare

Sringbok: The Okavango

POPPETS WITH PUPPETS

It's after half past three, grandchildren on the go
They want to entertain me and do a puppet show
One has a fine grey mole, another has a rabbit
A third a huge giraffe which has a nodding habit
They've written out the script, some lines are said by all
Like the introductory welcome and the final curtain call

In between times they go surfing on cushions from the couch
The puppet workers moving them from their hidden crouch
Mole says 'That's a good one,' rabbit glides ahead
While giraffe is standing tall and still nodding his head

Giraffe says 'I'm so tired, I've decided to go home'
The others say the same and suddenly there's a groan
From a mystery savage dog, an unwanted intruder
(in truth used at the front door as a draught excluder)

The puppet show is over, the workers take a bow
Rubbing their young biceps: they're all quite tired now.

ACTION STATIONS!

IN PATIENT WORLD - AND ESCAPE!

An interesting collection of people here in Lundy
The orthopaedic ward where I've been since Sunday
Four of us, all female, have replacement hips
One Left, three Right (like me) now we have to get to grips
With ritual exercising in spite of all the pain
Master frames, then crutches, till we walk again

One lady's diabetic, another needs transfusing
A third has a bad heart - this must be quite confusing
For the staff who are administering appropriate medication
As well as minding well their orthopaedic dedication
The orthopaedic surgeon is communicative and charming
Handsome, fit and talented, really quite disarming
More importantly his skills are just second to none
I know - sixteen years ago, I had the Left one done!

Members of his team come from round the world
One an Indian guy called Shiva, another dark and curled
An Iraqi man called Ben with manner courteous and kind
Was leaving the next day for General Practice 'grind'
In Halifax in Yorkshire, I said 'It makes a great career'
With his listening skills and manner, he'll have nothing to fear

In spite of scattered origins of professional staff
There seemed a camaraderie which made them joke and laugh
The nurses varied greatly, some 'bank' ones were in white
A couple needed wash and spin, one had quite a fight
With the regular staff of longterm registration
Recognised in blue and loyal to their station
Health-caring assistants, fat, thin, young and old
All pleasant and so helpful while doing as they're told

One such came from Turkey, her English was distinguished
She had an English husband: their children are good linguists
Then there was dear Fabio, night 'staff', Italian, 'bank'.
Young, flamboyant, attractive, accented, verbal prank
His jaunty walk unhurried, remarks casual, throwaway
Stirred ladies' pulses faster than they'd beat for many a day!

And what about the company? This is a female ward
Two more admitted now, not to be ignored
They're for hips tomorrow when three should be dismissed
Including Torrington Margaret with whom I reminisced
Hilary is a redhead, a chunky cheery maid
Who's trying to give up smoking but the habit's been her trade
For many a long year, since school, the wild fifth form
But with PC climate changes, she's trying to conform

And now today it's my turn to prepare for leaving here
Daughter Wendy will collect me and my in-patient gear
Then she's going to stay and keep an eye on me
Till first son Richard comes for continuity
The family have been great, supportive non-intrusive
Pre-op, three weeks with Charles, free B and B inclusive!
Helen's rung from India, from experience she'll remember
For she supervised that other hip, '91 September

As someone pointed out, what e'er their gift or facet
If families live on long enough, they can become an asset!

RECOVERY

TYING AND TRIMMING

I'm doing really well
At recovery's paces
Today I bent enough
To do my right shoe laces
(I need to wear these lace-ups
Echo in design
Arthritic feet are not replaced
At least not at this time!)

I did a bit of gardening
By the front lawn bedding
Crutch held in the left hand
Right hand for dead-heading

When I go to town
Courtesy of neighbours
Acting as my chauffeurs
And doing other favours,
It's great to see my friends
And sense my world again
It seems almost a lifetime
Since I took up my pen

Constant pain is wearing
Depressing, enervating
Post-operative relief
So exhilarating.

WHAT A RIDE!

Today's the first of August
I blew the sun a kiss
After all that rain
This summer warmth is bliss

I thought I might just try
To cut the waiting grass
Aboard the ride-on mower
But thought again, alas
Perhaps I ought to linger
And give this hip more time
Before I overdo things: -
I poured a glass of wine!

Dutch courage made me strong
I found the fuel, lead-free
Filled the empty tank
And had a talk with me
We decided to get going
It started up first time
I backed out of the barn
Along the tarmac line

Oh joy of joys, how wonderful
A happy engine rumble
It purred for three short hours
Through the lawns and jungle
A dear supportive friend
A properly trained nurse
Had said, 'I shouldn't do that'
But my hip feels none the worse

I believe the body tells you
When to stop or start
Nature's been around for ever
Very practised in her art.

WEIGHTLESS!

Today I've had a swim
Not in the tidal sea
Where waves would knock me over
And undercurrents be
Dragging me to right and left,
But in the local friendly pool
With changing rooms new-painted
In turquoise fresh and cool

Unlike the sandy beaches
The floor stays strong and steady
(I will return to shore again
When I'm good and ready)

The water was just lovely
Not chilly, not too warm
Giving effortless support
To my fumbling form
This experiment in movement
Lets me feel more normal
Than sets of exercises
Regimental, formal.

THE HIDDEN NOTE

The Piano Tuner came today
To my neglected Lipp
And soon I'll love to play
The pedals with new hip

An ivory had been missing
From the keyboard's towers
An 'F' around the middle
And I must have spent hours
Searching for this precious note
Which knew well how to hide
But well-practised Nevin Scott
Found it snuggling deep inside.

BACK INTO THE REAL WORLD

'Would you come and do your poetry on July the 24th
At the WI in Loxhore, with guests, so on, so forth?'
'Well,' I said, 'I'd love to but it will be just two weeks
After scheduled hip replacement to banish pain and creaks
So I will not be driving but to be there would be fine,'
Sheila said, 'Leave it to me: I'll ring nearer the time.'
So just after 6, Michael collected me,
Husband of member Ivy who knew how it would be
For they'd both had hip replacements
With good mobility

Loxhore's a lovely hamlet with close community
Where friendly faces greeted and then escorted me
As I crutched up to the garden with lay-out classical and neat
Tall Sunflowers, varied Cornflowers and Osteospermum treat
Host and hostess, Rob and Rosie (knew my neighbours
up the road!)
Rosie served strawberries and cream in true summer evening
mode
Rob assumed the role of barman and poured a sparkling glass
Most of us had more than one, as it came to pass!

He then moved on to cutting grass, - well it was the rarest of fine
eves
And Carole did the cork-popping with a certain expertise
She'd also made meringues, so light they gave a lift
(And shortbread I received as a 'thank you' gift)

The secretary did her bit and read the summer list
Of this year's diary dates - some should not be missed
She was well-informed on other things such as
Osteospermum names, and new hip ops in cars!

I sat on a good chair in the setting sun
Did my bits of poetry for a half hour run
Occasional extraneous noises like the grass machine
Women's warmth of chatter and the cork-popping queen
And one sad glass which shattered - I was surprised there were
not more
Easy to miscalculate on the terrace floor
These sounds so much enhanced ambience and atmosphere
Which I know will linger long in memory's inner ear

But generally it went well, for me especially well
My first proper outing since the hip in-patient spell
A lady called Jill Watts gave vote of thanks and praise
(A long ago connection from Family Planning days!)
Another man of substance, Peter, was my 'back to base' taker
Husband of dear Sheila, with life-giving pacemaker

It was all very special, back in the real world
New faces, conversation, responsive brain unfurled
Thank you for your generosity, and swelling charity's purse
By your practical response in buying up the verse!

RUBBISH RIDE

No driving for six weeks
That's the golden rule
An accident, tho' not my fault
At the least I'd be a fool
For disobeying advice
Of professionals who know
How most patients progress,
Take the average, fast or slow

I needed to take rubbish
Down to the front road
I'd done some gentle turning out
In convalescent mode
Hence the bags were very heavy
No way could I convey
Them while on crutches
To the refuse loading bay

Sometimes someone calls
At moments opportune
And I'm not above using them
They can be a boon
Put my rubbish sacks in bins
Move the poultry run
But today nobody came
And the job had to be done

So with black bags in the boot
I started up the car
And drove the vehicle down the drive
It isn't very far
And anyway it's private land
I dumped the rubbish thus
In its proper place
For the dustcart omnibus

(Another little notch
On convalescent's tree
Truly I could drive right now
But I won't - no, honestly!)

BACKWARD GLANCE

Thanks for having me to stay
When friends knew who I needed
So that to their good advice
I acquiesced and heeded

Eight weeks on, I'm looking back
And hindsight lets me see
With fresh appreciation
How much you've done for me

Three weeks' board and lodge
The mind on new vacation
In planet morphine's state
Before the operation

Grandchildren in the evening
Therapeutic a distraction
Homework and clarinet
For the music faction

Hospital admission
Mid-summer ward of heat
Post-op luxury handling
And soaking of the feet

I reflected on the surgery
Sawing mode prosthetic
I wouldn't want to hear that
Thank God for anaesthetic!

Collected by a daughter
And taken home to roost
Her care in my surroundings
A convalescent boost

Her youngest girl came with her
(She'd been under the weather)
And brought her sums and drawing
We studied them together

Her mother helped me bath
Massaged my tired back
Purposeful and strong
Sacrospinalis track

Then a son came with a daughter
Ellie, a lovely lass
Brought encouragement and company
But also cut the grass!

Prayers and calls from India
Clear long-distance line
From daughter who remembers
Caring here last time

Successful hip replacement
With supportive family blessed
And an orthopaedic surgeon
Of the very best!

Hip-op happy: crutches ahoy!

ANIMAL COMFORTS

SCHWAPPATS GONE!

I keep guinea fowl
They make a 'schwappat' noise
Unique and quite distinctive
They have a certain poise
They meander in a body
Grazing vegetarian
The odd fresh water toddy
Before a drop ovarian

The eggs are really splendid
Not large, with concrete shell
Deep yolk, slim white, good flavour
Which is the tale they tell
Of picking varied diet
Laying where they please
One after the other
I watch to get the wheeze
Of their latest nesting site
Which moves each week or so
From rosebed to the rockery
Then sneaky broad bean row

Now I know they are a hassle
But their 'schwappat' has a use
More alarming than the labrador
Who does have the excuse
Of being slightly deaf

And then there are the eggs
When they start to lay
Just ideal for Madeira cakes
Omelettes and soufflé

Grandchildren love the feathers
Exotic, mottled grey
Make collages at school -
So you'll understand I rue the day
When in broad daylight on a Sunday afternoon
A fox took not one, but three
Glennies to their doom

I'd shut them up at night
For fear of such a thing
Truly daylight robbery
How I miss their schwappat sing,
- never mind the eggs!

Chester

NO CHOICE

Chester is a Labrador, short-legged but pedigree
Black as the ace of spades, comforting company
He came my way by accident via my daughter who had been a
Friend of previous owners, Beverley and Cristina
Who were then returning to retire in Argentina

They brought him one weekend, he climbed out of the car
Stood and studied the estate, then like Olympic star
Raced round and round the lawn, then stopped and really smiled
- oh yes, he did, I saw him: excitement made him wild
If I'd had any doubts about giving him a home
They disappeared like mist before a rising sun

Cristina was delighted, in fact she shed a tear
Through which she smiled like the dog - emotions upped a gear
So Chester, Labrador, short-legged, came to live with me
I talk to him, he listens. I know he will agree.

ABIDING SHEEP

A Devon Longwool octave makes my hobby flock
Arusha is the strongest, of short-legged stubby stock
Plumped into a cushion of Afro-fashioned fleece
A teased out curling staple springs back upon release

Floreana is a gentler soul, a patchwork of a face
With features finely painted like a film of Breton lace
She's hesitant and timid, as was her ovine mother
But when the ram arrived, she made an ardent lover

Isabella's very feminine, a Barbara Cartland frothy
She shelters ostentatiously inside the north field bothy
A carping high-pitched bleat brings the rest to gaze -
She's only calling 'ewe' again: they drift away and graze

Serengetti, born the year I went to Tanzania
Strides like an ancient leopard through the plains of yesteryear
She is calm and full of wisdom and leads the flock to feed
On last year's parsnips, stringy greens, with just a hint of greed

Malvena, an adventurer, edged through my Steptoe fence
To join the Cluns next door for greener grass and thence
Across the road where ivy draped a painted pale
Wolfed the powerful poison: here ends her deadly tale

Belinda is a beauty, soft-fleeced, wide-eyed and cream
She tempts the Suffolk ram to boil a head of steam
The teasing-in-between time give a passionata trouble
But on sunny Easter Sunday, she proudly drops a double

Sallylightfoot: Devon Longwool ewe

Sallylightfoot named after Darwin's islands' crab
Has a somewhat sideways gait and the gift of bleating gab
Her tone is quite melodious, a comfort in the dark
When the vixen weirdly calls for her partner's mating bark

And finally there's Viney, a frumpy matron now
With heavy legs and limping, tousled wool and furrowed brow
But she's a well-tried lady, slung low with her fourth lamb
With the confident control she attested with the ram

There's a prevalent opinion, here and sometimes abroad
That sheep are dim and stupid, quite boring and quite bored
Someone might say of humans, 'They're like a flock of sheep'
In my book that's a compliment, for sheep their counsel keep!

FAMILY MATTERS

A LIFE INSIDE

How long was his life?
- As long as we remember
Accomplished in the warm
Of a womb one soft September

First movements brought great joy
Enhanced anticipation
Then disturbed with super strength
A drowning desperation

He was born completely still
A stillbirth to the world
Body beautiful, complete
A wisp of hair that curled

He saw none of the people
Very few saw him
And yet we hurt with loss
Grief flowing from the brim

In mind he'll live for ever
In the brightness of the dawn
A glowing evening sunset
A lamb just newly born

A swallow may fly early
Leave the milling flock
Mount a soaring thermal
Leave a life in hock

No one is ever lost
Intangible an essence
Lingers gently on
A comfortable presence.

THE LINK

You can't replace a baby
But desperate for another,
A little boy or girl
For Freddie, elder brother
Who'd been sad and disappointed
After the preparation
For sharing family life,
Sibling initiation,

His parents tried again,
Mother began to swell.
They hid their fresh anxieties
And did their best to quell
Those of Freddie, so aware
Of what had gone before
But children, rightly curious
Need to know the score.

So one day, he stood,
Hands on hips, mouth in a pout
'Mum you are big, when is
This baby coming out?'

Smiling, she said, 'quite soon'
(Hoping it would live)

'Well let's hope it doesn't die
Like the last one did!'

She found her smile was broadening
And then she really laughed -
'Oh Freddie, through it all
You're my life-saving raft!'

SUMMER BABY

I love you Isabella
Arousing protection
My tenth little special
Genetic connection

You're neat and compact
Hungry for life
A joyous relief
For my son and his wife

To hold you is bliss
For me such a wonder
Stirs me to tears
And also to ponder
How most babies come
Safely, intact
Yet this couple know
What it's like to be racked
By deep disappointment
Of George whom they lost
A salutary phase
An emotional cost

Today sees a new moon
In silver clear sky
Heralding summer
Raise spirits high

So welcome dear girl
To the spring of your days
My darling beginner
With love-winning ways.

MORTAL LINKS

A generations outing, a brilliant day in March
Granny, eldest daughter, daughter's daughter, Lily Darch
They walk the quay at Hartland, spy a Fulmar's nest
(Lily is just three years old and talks her very best)

They picnic in a field upon the family rug
And spread out all the goodies from the ancient family trug
Later they hike to Stoke, view the churchyard stones
And read historic glimpses of long-disjointed bones

Mother's finger trace the letters, wind-smoothed and lichen green
Dispel the granite's fetters to read who may have been
Head, foot and body stones with heavy load beneath
Of fatal births and fevers and shipwreck-stricken grief

Her voice is low, respectful with eternal fascination
Which attends the ends of others' lives, their final destination
She and Granny quietly muse upon the graveyard scene
Forget just for a moment, their charge, the Lily queen

They hear a plainsong voice, see her touch a stone
And make out she is reading as her mother's done
'I'm sorry you are dead and cannot see your friends
But when you're bad you all get killed and that is how it ends'

Amazed, they gazed at Lily
Stunned to silence, well almost
'Holy Mother' Granny said
Lilly's mother, 'Holy Ghost!'

FAMILY FORTUNE

Some family were staying
The weather dull and grey
Too cold to ride their bikes
Down the drive that day

Entertainment needed
So out came crayons and paper
Some of it so old
That Genevieve just gaped, her
Puzzled frown quite spoiling
The six year old's wide face
But she grabbed the largest piece
And made a table space

'I'm going to draw my family'
The others said 'How boring'
Her sister did some seagulls
Into blue space soaring

Her brother most predictably
Sketched a football pitch
(Granny'd time to make the lunch
With no distraction hitch)

All settled for just half an hour
To draw each masterpiece
The three were good, imaginative, - but
Gen's stays on a longer lease

It's on my kitchen door
Depicting centrally
Her adored elder sister
The blonde, long-legged Lily

My Family: an artist's impression!

Her brother, drawn, big-eared
In Arsenal shirt O2
Is saying 'I love Lily'
Which he's not inclined to do!
Lily winces slightly
'You've not said that to me'
'No, but sometimes I think it'
Says Tom with loyalty

Her Dad is upright, smiling
(Not that often, truth be told)
And labelled clearly 'Trevor'
With stance upright and bold

Her mother, Wendy looks quite short
That's how she didn't grow
She has my 'little' genes
Just the way things are, you know

As for Gen's self-portrait
With Copgey and Muzzy, treasures
She's modestly petite
Less than Lily's hip she measures

But even less significant
In corner bottom right
Is this very small grey Granny
With bun, Genevieve's height

The hairstyle's diagnostic
And with hindsight retrospective
I marvel how a six year old
Can get things in perspective!

LINES ABOUT LINES

A bank holiday in August, the summer's very last
A birthday picnic lunch under August sun which cast
An optimistic glow upon the celebrations
Of family assembled from three generations
Being such a holiday the beach was fairly heaving
So that Granny (on her own) had trouble in perceiving
Which was her family cross rock and sand terrain
For naked mobile youngsters all look so much the same

The daughter-in-law was spotted (she's elegant and tall)
Who simultaneously saw Granny (she's smaller than them all)
Thus united we enjoyed a memorable day
Bathing, tide just right, we surfed and swam the time away
The food was quite delicious, a veritable treat
Prepared by younger son, all I had to do was eat!

A granddaughter affectionate, sandy, dripping from the sea
Came and talked and then sat down on sandy dripping me
'I think Gina looks like you' said my son's in-law brother
Gina got up smartly, said she'd rather look like mother!
This was not unreasonable for as I've indicated
Her mother's poise and beauty must not be underrated
Then Gina stood and studied me with concentrated frown
'I love you Granny but you have got lines all the way down!'

She looked at me from head to toe before giving this line
Which spoke the very truth and truly I don't mind
I know how I look, I've mirrors everywhere
Although I must admit I'm not inclined to wear
My specs when making up or putting up by bun
Concessions on reflections since passing 71!

THE LONG JOURNEY

It took nine months her passage, from beginning to the finish
It started unexpectedly which in no way should diminish
The triumph of survival through the darkness on the way
And the ultimate emergence into the light of day

The beginning was quite small, you might say microscopic
She forged her path relentlessly - static could mean ectopic
En route she found a cove, welcoming and warm
She wriggled in for comfort just before a violent storm

Here she grew in stature, fed gently by her host
Who would pat her at a distance and smile a quiet boast
She thought she'd stay for ever, tho she fancied larger quarters
Her limbs were folded up and in like some Darwinian tortoise

She listened to the music of the waters where she lay
And the voice of someone singing 'cross an ocean far away
These were sounds of comfort, of tenderness and love
And now and then seemed nearer, like a foot or two above

Then exactly forty weeks from the day of her creation
The walls around her cove moved with rhythm and gyration
She really couldn't linger, she thought she might have drowned
The force drove her head first, there was no time to turn round

She went onward with the flow, unhappy with the heat
The narrow route, the pressure, not something she'd repeat
Then it was over, she was free, there were people, quite a crowd
They all seemed much elated - did they have to talk so loud?

One shouted, 'It's a girl!' well she'd known all along
But just then she heard that music, this was her mother's song
Out in the wide world, solo, separate - and adored
But still plugged in, connected, by an everlasting chord.

ARC OF LIFE

Today I saw a rainbow
Full-arched, clear and bold
I remembered how you liked them
And vowed a pot of gold
Was at the end
Which end you never told!

The outer rim was red
So warm and wonderful
Reminded me of Christmas
When you held a bundleful
Of logs
For the open fire

The red merges into orange
Blurring the verging lining
With hues of special sunsets
Which go and leave us pining
For a sunrise
To bring another day

The yellow is a little shy
As an early primrose spring
Blinking in the pale sun
Like uncertainties you'd bring
Such as
Which ram to hire

Green has a naïve freshness
As a lawn's first sheen
Which as yet knows not
Of pests and grass machine
Like life
Which starts uncluttered
Only hindsight gives the theme
Of how
We might have changed things
And then what might have been

Autumn rainbow

Green's lining arc is blue
Compare a summer sky
Cloudless and for ever
Raising spirits high
Beyond the space of life
So we're not afraid to die.

Indigo comes next and links
This clarity of light
To the soft caress of evening
Which comes before the night

The so-called shrinking violet
Hugs the inside rim
Nestling with a closeness
Of a shadow's subtle whim

This completes the spectrum
A glorious combination
Of colours
From the outside in
A transient inspiration

Life reflects a rainbow
In colour, light and shade
Neither stays for ever . . .

When the strands begin to fade
We know the rainbow will return
With gentle showers and sun
- But the grieving is more lasting
When a loved one's life is done -

Whatever you believe
There is a desolation
But those who've been there know
There's also consolation

For
No one is ever lost
Intangible an essense
Lingers gently on
A comfortable presence

A COMFORTING CONNECTION

My favourite chair's a stool
Made of brass and wood
It hasn't travelled far
No reason why it should

It had another life
In a pub, the Exchange Royal
Where my husband drank
After routine daily toil

It stands quite tall, substantial
Like him, to tell the truth
They were a matching pair
And others knew, forsooth

The stool was his, but theirs
You know what I mean
Clients would ask the landlord
'Has John Tyler been?'

Had he not, they'd settle
For another deck
It was all polite and pleasant
With gentlemen's respect

The landlord at that time
Was a man John Pitts
His wife, dear Anne was mayor
Showed wisdom, wile and wits

So when the Pitts moved on
They gave to us this stool
Which still lives by my table
Under Tyler rule.

Now I'm on my own
I've inherited this piece
Tho a son would like it one day
Hence it's on uncertain lease

Grandchildren know the score
I must have it for my meals
One'll say 'You can't sit there
You know how Granny feels!'

I like its height and presence
Adjustable, that's true
And I wind it up a little
To get a better view

It's particularly useful
When friends come in for supper
Just that bit higher than the chairs
And helps me keep the upper
hand.

HOMEWARD FLIGHT
Sonnet for the swallows

I love the early daylight of September
When the mist and sunrise glow comfort the mind
With a soothing softness of the autumn kind
Which stills the heart, promotes me to remember
The morning when the swallows all departed
To follow in your wake when you had flown
Assembling all the week as if they'd known
The leaving process had already started
You longed to see the swallows in the spring
They brought the promise of the longer days
Collecting mud and insects on the wing
Endearing with their wise and winning ways
And now each September I recall
How they watched over you before the fall.

WHITE FOR REMEMBRANCE

Two white swans flew in for the first time ever
To grace my silent lake in grey November weather
I had no time to stand and stare, I blew them both a kiss
Then fled to Sunday church, this was the armistice

Red poppies on the crosses in the graveyard grass
Red poppies on the choirgowns, white wine for the Mass
Who are these arrayed in white? - Through great tribulation
Washed in red blood of the lamb: a final consecration

I thought of Uncle Leslie killed in World War I
At about nineteen I think and what it must have done
To his younger brother - my father still at home
And his father as well whom I've never known
Contakion sung with feeling, the Russian slant of story
Then silence, National Anthem, Land of Hope and Glory

After service, I came home, without the cup of tea
And strangely felt that Leslie was somewhere near to me
Until I saw the swans had upped and flown away
Then I knew he'd been and brought a friend to stay
For just a little while - all in white array . . .

We will remember them
At the going down of the sun
And on the morning after
While countless ages run.

Remembrance poppies

A HAPPY ENDING

We all knew you were dying
Yet you filled our lives with laughter
With honeyed reminiscences
Like things that happened after
The pubs had closed

Much I had forgotten
It was good that you remembered
Precious pleasant memories
In full and not dismembered
Before you dozed

I looked forward to the midday
When you were most alert
And life was briefly normal
Till your body hurt
And needed medication

Your whole life was special
For the children and for me
But these last weeks were magic
And will for ever be
A consolation

You left us quietly in peace
And everyone was smiling
Of course we wept as well
But an ambience quite beguiling
Kept us calm

Thank you for being here
And sharing out your life
Your presence lingers near
Dispersing stress and strife
A reassuring balm.

ANNO DOMINI

LOW FOOTING

I simply love high heels and as I'm rather short
(5'2" in stocking feet) I've generally bought
Smart shoes that give me height, elevate my gaze
Into other's eyes and over broader ways

I had quite a collection in every shade of leather
My favourite - French - in yellow, footlight as a feather
I was happy with my shoes, felt tall enough and neat
Two inches gave me confidence to stand on my own feet

But at a wedding in Slovakia, when we danced all through the
night
And sang to local music and got a little tight
And discarded all the footwear amidst the stepping babel
And then the tights and stockings to footsie 'neath the table -

I suddenly felt pain under all my toes
Sharp, excruciating, oh nobody knows!
No longer could I dance at all, I sat and smiled, so brave
But in reality I felt like two feet in the grave

And that was the beginning of my indisposition
A hampering of mobility, a mandatory submission
To ageing of important joints called osteoarthritis
Permanent, progressive, not temporary like phlebitis

So I had a consultation with the man who did my hips
Which I must say have been wonderful, enabling all my trips
To glorious foreign parts to climb and raft and camp
With no rusting or discomfort in spite of all the damp

He was welcoming, concerned, said, 'I did good jobs there'
(Put my hips through all their paces) and truly I concur
However on the other hand he had much less to say
You just can't replace feet, maybe they will one day

I had supports and tablets, he said 'See how it feels'
Frankly not much better, and I can't wear my high heels!
To resist the strong temptation, the best have left this home
For elder daughter Wendy, sadly something of a clone.

Footnote: Today I saw a young man who used to be a punk
             I said, 'My how you've grown'
             But I think it's me who's shrunk!

A CHANGE OF VIEW

I've always thought dependency
Might just show a tendency
Not to be an independent soul
But as the years tick by
And I become less spry
I might assume
A more dependent role

When well-meant help is offered
And timely support proffered
I'm learning to accept it with good grace
When the bookcase fell apart
A neighbour, bless his heart
Mended it
And stood it on its base

A lamb tumbled as it ambled
Got bogged down and tight-brambled
In the spillway underneath the bridge
I endeavoured to retrieve it
Struggled long, you must believe it
But had to phone a farmer
To pull it up the ridge

Then there was the beech tree
It fell to nearly reach me
In the strongest of the February gales
My heart was near to breaking
But this undertaking
Was all cut up and cleared
By a man from Wales

When I struggle with the shopping
With some limping and some lopping
An unexpected Sherpa is a blessing
So I no longer whine or whelp
I just accept the help
It's usually a man
- That's a bonus I'm confessing!

LIFESPAN

Life is far too short
I've so much still to do
And time is running out
For all, no matter who
They might be

But now I'm over seventy
A reasonable lifespan
I have less time than some
And need to fill it while I can
Prioritise

People must come first
Family, neighbours, friends
Those who share my interests
Gardening, music, drama trends
Communications

I love to do some scribbling
For the Writers' group
Where we share impressions
Through a common loop
New creations

I'm presently content
While I purposefully coast
Thankful for life's offers
Of which I make the most
With gratitude.

DORA'S CONSOLATION

She lived in a one-bedroomed flat
And held a garden in her head
Her carer said 'Just fancy that'
To Dora's 'The Daffodils are dead'

It was indeed the spring
Wordsworth's blooms abounded
But not seen three storeys up
Social worker was astounded

Earlier she'd talked of Snowdrops
Said they were white and pure
Muttering 'Unlike this Indian helper
Whom I have to endure'

She raved about the Bluebells
'They are my favourite flower.
I'm walking through my wood
Of trees that trail and tower'

The carer nodded
To the District Nurse
Dora seemed to her quite mad
She was definitely worse

'I've planted red Geraniums
In all the flower pots
And white ones at the back
In several different lots'

'How lovely' said the vicar
In voice gentle and dutiful
She didn't want communion
But sang
'All things bright and beautiful'

'The Dahlias are out
Some have lovely dark red leaves'
The carer frowned, the doctor said
'It's fine - just what she sees.'

So Dora's year progressed
Through seasonal garden plantias
Rhododendrons, Cistus
Antirrhinums and Astrantias
Helleniums and Euphorbias
Poppies by the score
Gazanias and Godetias
And many many more

Rheum and Rodgersia
Iris and Skunk Cabbage
Gunnera she said from
The son of Mrs Babbage

Then one night she talked of Roses
Her favourite one was red
She 'held' one in her hand
And placed it on the bed
Then picked it up again
Smelled with imagination
Said that it was fading
To its final destination

She smiled contentedly
And 'laid' it on the cover
When the morning dawned
Like her Rose, her life was over

The Indian helper sensed the silence
And scrambled to her toes
For a moment she was sure she saw
On the quilt, a faded Rose.

Gunnera, 'laid to rest' for the winter: Rosemoor

DREAMING AND SUPPOSING

AN AWAKENING

I dream very little
By days or by nights
In fact I am quite jealous
Of minds which take such flights
I have a friend who lost her man
The same year end as me
And she dreamed of him constantly
Her joy was plain to see

She'd relay all the detail
Just normal situations
Tho some sounded quite far-fetched
Perhaps her dream creations
I thought I might compete
And fabricate a dream
Of something I'd enjoyed
Somewhere we had been

But before this was perfected
And ready for the telling
I had a dream for real one night
Of substance quite compelling
John used to do the man tasks
In the garden and you'd see
Him chop down trees and cut the grass
- After - some such fell to me

I'm not good with machinery
But mastered the ride-on mower
After one or two small crashes
And scratching the barn door
So I had this dream
I was cutting down the drive
And quarrelled with a conifer
And nearly took a dive.

We'd had some heavy showers
Front wheel caught in mud and muck
I tried reverse manoeuvre
But was well and truly stuck
Suddenly dear John appeared
All casual and smiling
Said 'Oh dear, what a cock-up!'
In soft tones quite beguiling.

He just pushed the machine
It slid gently back
He disappeared, I carried on
And finished off the track

What is really strange
I swear there's now a mark
On the dreamed-of conifer
A stretch of damaged bark
This reminds me of his coming
And to take more care
I don't think I need dreams
I know he's here and there . . .!

DIRECTIONS

A signpost in the road
At Opportunity Cross
Whichever route you choose
Could be your gain or loss

Some go down Lovers' Lane
Though they have one safe at home
But a fluid roving eye
Excites into a foam
Of irresistible desire
Which seduces them to roam

The Garden Route's attractive
Flowers drawn between the letters
Just a short walk to the Centre
Where the scents can fell the fetters
Of privet-hedged suburbia
And next door's carping betters

The arrow to the school
Is daubed with yellow paint
In rough outlines of chickens -
Really clever and quite quaint
A young mum knows this trademark
Her Thomas is no saint
She'll travel on with him
Till he becomes a man
And on his own departs from home
To paint a living if he can

To the east it says 'Town Centre'
Quite a walk, a narrow road
Without a proper pavement
So mind the Highway Code
Face oncoming traffic
To be seen and to see
Difficult with all the bends
But that's how life can be

The sign to the King's Arms
Is red in cloak and face
The barmaid there's accustomed
To the landlord's fond embrace
Tom's father goes there often
He likes the strong draught beer
Tom's mother says in several ways
The cost is far too dear

The sign to St John's church
Embossed with a small cross
The gutters sporting gargoyles
Walls softened with green moss

So:-
If you want a lover
You know which way to go
If you must outdo the neighbour
Try the garden show

If your little one's at school
At just turned half past three
You meet him, with the baby
And all go home for tea

Saturday's the day
For the centre of the town
Shopping in the morning
Walking up and down
Chatting with the locals
A community's mixed bunch
Popping in the King's Arms
For the Ploughman's lunch

Sunday is the Sabbath
A few will go to church
Others view the graves
And watch the pigeons perch

Life is what you make it
At whatever stage
And rests on your directions
Independent of your age!

THE DAY BEGAN LIKE THIS

I woke early which was strange
For not much disturbs my slumber
I lay and listened for the reason
Heard the rumble of the rumba

I recognised the beat
(I remember proper dancing
When we took a partner
Unlike today's lone prancing)

It re-awakened memories
Of youth's own yesteryear
And dancing through the night
When life was fresh and clear

My heart took up the rhythm
My feet began to tingle
It even brought to minmd
A '50's rumba jingle

I enjoyed it all so much
I didn't question for a while
From whence the music came
In such compelling style

I recalled my long red dress
With brave décolletage
Flaunting unashamedly
To all the world at large

I journeyed this nostalgia
And rode on till the dawn
Brought sweeping through the room
A breathtaking summer morn

With the light, the music stopped
Abruptly, - then I found
I'd only dreamed I'd been awakened
By seductive rumba sound

Somehow it didn't matter
This had been a special way
For me - magical and comforting
To start another day.

DARK PASSAGE

The moon called in for coffee
Not here but down the road
That runs direct from my house
Towards the sun's abode
He swung his dark cloak silently
And stunned the sun to night
She was desperate to be seen
As he blotted out her light

She was used to common clouds
One has to be in Devon
Adored a clear blue sky
Her personal seventh heaven
But this was deep disturbing
And took away her breath
A sense of total snuffing
Of doom, impending death

She shrank into a slim eclipse
Like meanest of new moons
But shot brief fiery glances
In reds and dark maroons
The earth was black as night
Birds puzzled, made for roost
The dog slumped into bed
Thousands watched it on the coast

The moon may have had discomfort
From the sun's bright searing light
For he didn't linger long
When she gleamed out to the right

Then it was all over!
Earth was light as day
The sun smiled through the clouds
The moon had passed away.

SMILE FIRST

The style of her smiling
Was strange
Brief but beguiling
To a range
Of men of all ages

The lad with the papers
The man with the milk
The hopeful MP
Who wore ties of silk
And kept birds in cages

The newborn baby
Next door
And his father forlorn
And quite poor
With a dog who liked barking

She charmed the headmaster
Quite clearly
He sometimes smiled back
- well nearly
When he'd finished his marking

The vicar was tall and
Begowned
Not for his humour
Renowned
But she made him laugh

A man in the old people's
Home
Who'd shrunken with age
To a gnome
They had it on file
He never did smile
Then he did - to her – not the staff

So where did it come from
This smile?
Catchy enough
To beguile
Any man
It crinkled her face
Like a fine Breton lace
In the sun.

She'd been born 'neath a slinky
New moon
And slithered out swiftly a fortnight
Too soon
-    So they said
From her life's early start
She discovered the art
Of being ahead.

RHYME WITH REASON

I'd like to write a poem which wins a competition
I sent one in some time ago, a last-minute submission
Which got 'highly commended' 'and made me full of hope
But that was just a 'one-off' and I'm not sure how to cope
With thinking of a theme which gets to judges' hearts
As well as to their intellect and to their other parts

The ones which win most often seem to be blank verse
I remember one long sad piece all about a nurse
Another with an oak tree as its steadfast title
With language deep and strong and every nuance vital
I've tried to write blank verse and read out one or two
One of my Writers' Group said, 'Stick to what you can do!'

I like to write with rhythm and associated rhyming
I find the two together assist the crucial timing
'Real' poets studying amateurs seem to look with pity
On these trends, tend to call them 'doggerel' and 'ditty'
I like the Poet Laureate, Andrew Motion, his blank verse
But I also love John Betjeman with rhyming tight and terse
Amusing and accessible, easy to recall
- I'm going to struggle on with what I'm best at after all!

BITS OF HEAVEN

CHURCH FÉTE

Today St Michael's and All Angels holds its summer fête
With furling flags and competitions and cheap cream teas as bait
The sun shines bright and warm throughout this July day
For the morning preparations and the afternoon make hay

The grass has all been manicured, quite short carpet-cropped
And trees with trailing branches, trimmed and lightly lopped
This is the vicarage garden's day for tho hardly flower-bordered
It must think 'someone cares to make me look so ordered'

A woman of some substance gives the opening words
High up from the balcony with breathing space and birds
She is the new headmistress at our local senior school
Earned respect already, some pupils think her 'cool'

There's something here for everyone of any age and taste
They clamour for the home-made cakes with nigh indecent haste
Previous keepers of the books, secondhand but some look new
Frown flicker at the lay-out, but I see they've bought a few

I carry a small camera as often is my wont
And take a sitting couple, they pose, she says 'Oh don't!'
At the crucial moment I hear a tell-tale 'zing'
The film (on 39) is spent . . . . I quickly change the thing
The vicar's wife espies me, 'could you do the photo stint?
We'll sell them in the Red Cross shop at 50p a print.'

So I advance with camera to study all the stalls
The new young bookstall vendors, - (I bought songs from Music
                                                                        Halls)
Bric-a-brac and draw with earnest ladies writing
A selection of fine prizes which makes it more exciting

A farmer on the Skittles copes with the children's queue
A good scene for a photograph so I'm tempted and take two
The plants are quite impressive, neat-potted, moist and labelled
Managed by an expert who's been a while disabled
The organist does the hoop-la, mostly youthful players
Whose size dictates the distance, some really need a dais

A novelty idea I hadn't come across
10p to hold a rabbit, guinea pig or mouse
The children seem to love this, cuddling with a gentle touch
As they do to see the dog show, more interesting than Crufts
They can also ride a donkey, suddenly grow tall
See how they'll see as parents, looking down on all

The Optician as White Rabbit, paints the children's faces
As if they've just flown in from other planets, worlds and places
A smaller surface covered in careful operation
By the vicar's daughter painting nails in hues of rare sensation

Food is in abundance, fresh baking, the cream teas
A draw for lovely strawberry cakes, cold ice creams to please
In contrast to the barbecue - for hotter palates caters
Managed with experience on impressive apparatus

All this and entertainment too, schoolchildren country dancing
To an instrumental small ensemble, really quite enchanting

A day to remember, to store in memory's search
Lots of the people present are seldom seen in church
And yet they seem to need us for life's special dates
Like births, marriages and deaths and especially summer fêtes

PS: The sitting couple's picture, (39th) - I had some doubt
        (A pair of retired metics) - only 'oh don't' came out!

SITTING SIFAKA

Oh you beautiful creature, protected and content
How you protect each other, on family closeness bent
So lithe and agile, leaping from ground to tamarind
Then climbing without effort to join some kith and kin
And sway on overhanging branch of some nearby tree
Thus mimicking a man on a high wire circus spree

You preceded man by many a million years
Your feet are like his hands but it's man who's in arrears
You've maintained your bonding throughout that space of time
And kept tribal commitment like creatures in their prime
Your beauty is a legend from wide-eyed gaze so sweet
To coat of grey white velvet and ballet on two feet
You seem to dance for joy, perhaps your just reward
For hanging on monogamous to your genetic cord

One very early morning just at the break of day
I spied a sitting Sifaka in the sun's first ray
She held and fed her youngster with human pose quite scary
So that my thoughts were turned to the nursing Virgin Mary
To be anthropomorphic may be considered foolish
A misconceived analogy, even a little ghoulish
But that's how I'll remember you in memory's sharp measure
Where you'll remain imprinted for ever and for ever.

ECHOES OF EXMOOR

What is it about Exmoor
That moves the mind and heart?
Maybe it's royal history
King John played quite a part
Loving well the hunting
Centuries ago
(That pursuit now somewhat threatened
But I don't think it will go!)

Before that owned by Alfred
A man of brilliancy and brains
Whose constancy and planning
Thwarted all the Danes
(The only thing some know of him
Which quite unreasonably makes
Me sad about their ignorance -
He burnt some peasant's cakes!)

I digress, we must move on
To see this wooded weald
Looked after for six centuries
Royally blessed and sealed
Then disafforested
(So not a new phenomenon)
The moor remained for ponies, sheep
To graze their days upon

They come out of the heather
On bleak and misty morns
The ponies with proud prancing
The rams with handsome horns
There are birds and bees and butterflies
And rugged headlands decked
With flowers like thrift and samphire
But where also ships were wrecked

Some love the coastal footpaths
The narrow wooded coombes
Or the moorland outlaws fabled
In fiction's famous Doones
Legacy and legend
Pirate, highwayman and king
Threading through the ambience
But for me the thing -

Which makes it very special
Are visits of my life
Younger days with children
While still an early wife
And later when they'd all left home
With just my man and me
Now I sometimes go alone
Absorb tranquillity.

Grandchildren have the habit
Thanks to their parents' way
So I can tag along with them
When they come to stay.

ANTICIPATION

I'm close to the Antarctic, I'm underneath a world
Of white feathered skies above and gentle waves all pearled
With a fickle foam

A handsome black-browed Albatross is gliding into view
With a graceful sense of breeding and knowing what to do
And where to roam

Fin Whales blow their presence with forceful spurts of fountains
Then briefly show their strength as transient heaving mountains
Gleaming in the sun

Cape Petals weave about in the vessel's wake
Under, over, back and forth, as if to make
A pattern like their own

Other birds join in the theme, I've still to name so many
Keen twitchers point and recognise Wilson's Petrels, ten a penny
By colour and their motion

The skies all reach the sea from every point of view
Explorer II is here alone with passengers and crew
In a mighty ocean

Christmas Day has dawned, the first iceberg is viewed
On the port side of the ship, blue-shaded, shaped and hewed
By weather, wind and wave

This is very special, I find I'm near to tears
And this, just the beginning of an ice-scape formed through

                                                                    years

Into mountain, cove and cave

                    Then on to the Antarctic
                    With its special isthmus
                    So much to anticipate
                    But today is Christmas

The Blue Antarctic

COMMONS TIME

I dreamed a ream of Torrington
Of forty years ago
Where we picnicked with the children
Sweet lullaby and low

While the baby slept the afternoon
Her brothers fought a war
With sticks among the bracken
Black-bruised a Grass Snake's lore

Her sister gathered flowers
Speedwell and Celandine
And laid them by the infant
Oh communion cup divine

Sheep safely grazed on Commons land
By rights this town affords
From bounteous liberality
Bestowed by ancient lords

Echoes down the ages
Of Royalist rendez-vous
Of fires, chance and intended
A warmth of déjà-vu

Centuries of Commons
I dream them all as one
A thousand ages in their sight
Are like an evening gone

FRESH AIR

Each spring is better than the last
And takes me by surprise
When a soft wind blows its promise
Through pale blue cottoned skies
And shimmers Blackthorn's leaf-bared blossom
Shafts Primrose yellow light
Whispers dainty Daffodils
To launch a Brimstone flight

It stirs the long-grown winter lawns
And trees poised with buds on hold
Starlings waiting for their mating
Till sun warms grey to gold

In the long drear of short winter days
When Christmas and family have been
I fear the mind's dark cloud may never lift
To let the spring come in
Then the threshold of the changing season
Brings sharp anticipation
Of colour, light, revival
Rebirth, a new gestation

Each faithful spring is better than the last
And tho' I love the summer and the fall
I am convinced
Today at least
That my last spring will be the best of all

Spring!

FULL CIRCLE

My Granny, Hannah Mary,
Born eighteen seventy
In Devon's salty Salcombe
Near the clear Custom House Quay
Married young, a sailor
Who sailed the seven seas
In the handsome Adelaide Mary
Bringing citrus fruits to please

Her first son, Oscar, born at home
Weighed nigh eleven pounds!
The doctor came out late
On horseback on his rounds
No in-patient monitoring
No underwater birth
Granny's girlish waist
Assumed a grander girth!

They had six babes all told
Two died young and went to Heaven
But Oscar was the only one
Born in County Devon
For engines replaced sails
In bigger ships with funnels
Which spewed out smoke and steam
Foghorned across the gunwales

And such were built elsewhere
In special huge dry docks
In ports like Liverpool, my home
Where seagulls flew in flocks
So Granny had to move
To a back street terrace house
In the port of Liverpool -
But she never was a Scouse

My Granny: Hannah Mary

She kept her Devon accent
Until the day she died
And always talked of Devon
With longing, love and pride
People travelled little then
But she went back once - to be
Disgusted at the washing
Hanging out along the Quay!

I'm sad she died so long before
I came to live in Devon
No doubt somewhere she's pleased
I found her earthly Heaven

I loved the docks of Liverpool
Where my father toiled
But the waters of the Mersey
Got silted up and spoiled
The shipping went elsewhere
The buildings all converted
To upmarket apartments
Never to be reverted

After more than forty years
Of Torrington May Fair
And 'uz be plaized to see 'ee'
Strung out across The Square -
Tho I'll never be a 'local' . . .
This is home, my heart is here
Roll back two generations
And thank you Granny dear!